Adorable
Wearables
That Teach Early Concepts

by Donald M. Silver and Patricia J. Wynne

SCHOLASTIC
PROFESSIONAL BOOKS

New York • Toronto • London • Auckland • Sydney
Mexico City • New Delhi • Hong Kong • Buenos Aires

For Stephanie Lesmoine Mitchell

A true profile in courage
—PJW and DMS

Cover design by **Norma Ortiz**
Cover photography by **James Levin**
Cover and interior illustrations by **Patricia J. Wynne**
Interior design by **Holly Grundon**

ISBN: 0-439-22265-6

6 7 8 9 10   40   09 08

Contents

Introduction

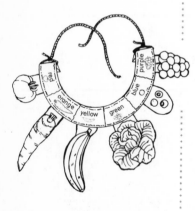

Welcome to *Adorable Wearables That Teach Early Concepts!* The twelve wearables and lessons in this book help teach the alphabet, colors, shapes, counting, senses, and more. As students build their understanding of key concepts, they will be practicing important skills such as observing, comparing, and classifying. The paper patterns and instructions make creating every wearable easy and fun. Additionally, many of the wearables include word or number labels that help increase children's vocabulary and improve developing language skills. Learning with wearables is sure to be both fun and educational for you and your students!

What's Inside
The wearable in each chapter focuses on a specific concept. The chapters are independent and can be used in any order. Featured within each are the following sections:

Wearable Illustration
This picture shows how the finished wearable looks. It can be helpful to use as a reference when making the wearable.

Skills
This section lists the skills children practice as they make and use the wearable.

Materials
Use the reproducibles and supplies noted in this section to make the wearables.

Building Vocabulary
Key vocabulary related to the chapter's topic and concepts is contained here. Use some or all of these words with the Teaching With the Wearable section, depending on the level of your students.

Making the Wearable
These easy-to-follow instructions include diagrams for assembling the wearables.

Teaching With the Wearable
This section provides a step-by-step lesson map for using the wearables to teach the chapter's primary concepts and skills.

Extending Learning
In this section you will find related activities to further students' skill development and understanding of basic concepts.

Book Links
Use the books listed in this section, which complement and build on the chapter's main concepts, as springboards for class discussion.

Try This!
These activities complement the lesson and provide fun opportunities to strengthen skills and broaden learning.

Helpful Hints for Making the Wearables

※ The thickest black lines on the reproducible pages are CUT lines.

※ Dotted lines on the reproducible pages are FOLD lines. When folding, be sure to crease well.

※ Some models have slits or holes that require cutting. An easy way to cut them is to fold the paper at a right angle to the solid cut lines. Snip along the lines from the crease of the fold inward.

※ Glue sticks can often be substituted for tape. However, some situations (for example, creating flaps) require tape. Thin tape is easier for students to apply to the models than thicker tape.

※ If students will be coloring the wearables and using tape, have them color first so they won't need to color over the tape.

※ If a single wearable will be handled a great deal, consider creating it from heavier paper. Simply glue the reproducible page onto construction paper before beginning assembly. Or, hand feed sheets of construction paper into a photocopier; the reproducible will print directly onto the heavier stock paper.

※ Some wearables are more challenging to assemble than others. Read through each Making the Wearable section (or make the wearable yourself) beforehand to determine if it's appropriate for your students to make that wearable on their own.

Shape-and-Pattern Crown

Students make a colorful crown to learn about shapes and patterns.

Skills

observing attributes of shapes

extending repeated patterns

Materials

☼ copies of reproducible pages 8–10 (for each student)

☼ scissors

☼ tape or glue sticks

☼ colored pencils, crayons, or markers (optional)

Making the Wearable

1. Have students cut out the crown segments and shape pieces.

2. Direct them to position the crown segments face up, as shown, and tape or glue them together end-to-end.

3. Have students match and then tape or glue the shape pieces to the pattern printed on their crowns. Tell children to set extra shapes aside.

4. Challenge students to finish the "Continue the pattern here" section on their crowns using the extra shapes. Remind children to follow the square-circle-square-circle pattern established.

Building Vocabulary

bigger
circle
longer
pattern
shorter
sides
smaller
square
triangle

5. Let children color their crowns, if desired.

6. Fit a crown around each student's head
    and tape in place.

Teaching With the Wearable

1. Have students observe and compare attributes
    of the shapes on their crown.

2. Ask children to name and describe each shape. Ask: *Is this shape made of
    straight or rounded lines? If it has straight lines, how many sides does it have?
    Are the sides all the same length? How are these two shapes similar? Different?*

3. Invite students to wear their crowns during a special time each day,
    such as snack or circle time.

1, 2, 3 Shapes by Gayle
Bittinger (Totline
Publications, 1994).
Activities, games,
music, and art help your
students learn about
all kinds of shapes.

··●● Extending Learning ●●··

Patterning 101

Help students strengthen patterning skills by discussing and
identifying the shape patterns on their crowns. As they may
notice, the crown template has two different patterns: The headband
follows a square/circle/square/circle pattern. The crown's points follow
a small triangle/large triangle/small triangle/large triangle pattern. As
students discuss the patterns, introduce other simple patterns, such as
ABABAB, ABBABB, and ABCABC.

Shape I-Spy

Have students put on their crowns and look around the classroom
for objects with the same shape outlines they used in their crown
patterns (square, circle, triangle). A clock might have a circle outline.
A desk might have a rectangle outline. Discuss how the shapes are
alike (the square and rectangle have 4 sides) and different (a triangle
has three sides, etc.). Take this activity further by inviting students to
point out patterns on their clothing, in the block center, and so on.

Try This!

Have a shape
parade! Invite
your students to
wear their crowns
and go on a parade
down the hall and out
to the playground.
Draw giant outlines
on the asphalt with
chalk. Then, challenge
students to march
in line along the
outlines to trace
the shapes on their
crowns. Be sure to
point out the
straight or curved
lines of each shape
(circle, square,
triangle).

Shape-and-Pattern Crown

tape or glue

tape or glue

8

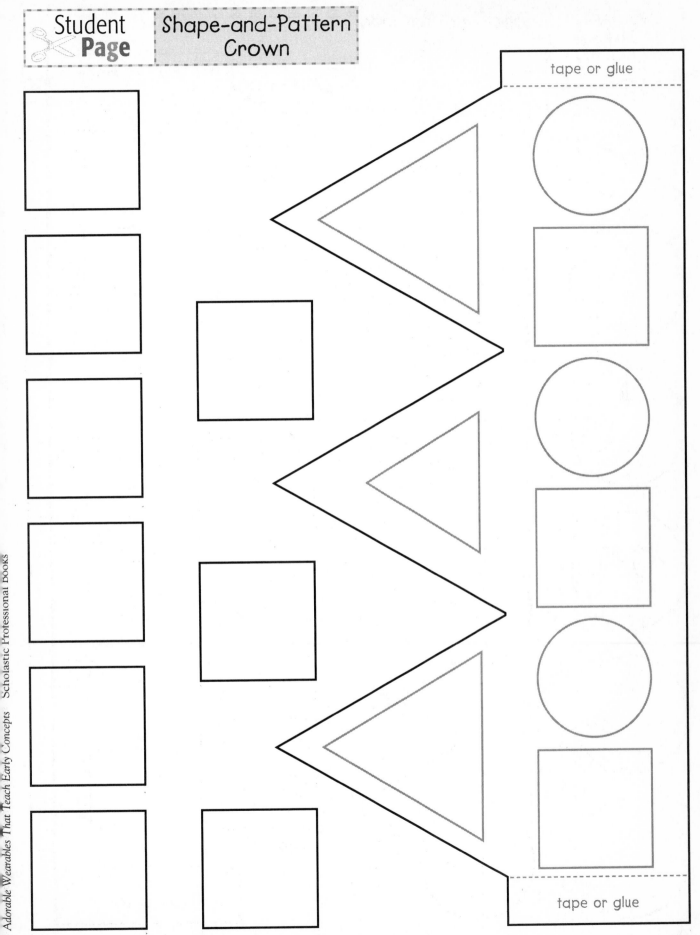

tape or glue

tape or glue

9

tape or glue

Continue the pattern here.

tape or glue

Adorable Wearables That Teach Early Concepts   Scholastic Professional Books

Size-Sorting Apron

Students make an apron with pockets for sorting big and small pictures.

Skills

observing
comparing
sorting
classifying

Materials

☀ copies of reproducible pages 13–16 (for each student)

☀ scissors

☀ tape

☀ brown paper bag (for each student)

☀ 3-foot-long piece of yarn (for each student)

☀ colored pencils, crayons, or markers (optional)

Making the Wearable

Guide children in following these directions:

1. Color the pictures and pockets, if desired.

2. Cut out the pictures and apron pockets. Set them aside.

3. Cut the front panel from a paper bag. In the steps that follow, this panel will become an apron.

4. Lay the panel flat. Fold a crease down one long side that is one-and-a-half inches wide.

5. Place the yarn along the inside of the folded panel. The loose ends of yarn should extend beyond the ends of the fold. Tape the fold in place.

6. Flip the panel over, so the taped fold is facedown. Position the apron pockets side by side. Tape them to the panel by applying tape on three sides, leaving the top of each pocket open and functional.

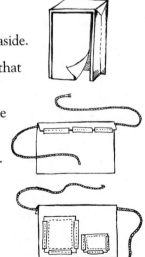

Building Vocabulary

•••●◗ ◖●•••

apron
big
bigger
different
pocket
same
small
smaller
sort

11

Book Links

A Pig Is Big by Douglas Florian (Greenwillow, 2000). The author's rhyming verses and colorful illustrations make this book about sizes a BIG delight.

Try This!

Invite children to sort big and small handprints. Begin by cutting five-inch squares of paper, enough for every student to have two. Tell each child to pick which palm he or she would like to print. Then paint it with tempera paint. (It tickles!) Ask each student to press the paint-covered hand onto a paper square. Then, send one of the blank squares home with every student. Attach a note inviting families to make a big, grown-up sized handprint their child can use to sort. Children will have BIG fun identifying which handprint is small (theirs) and which print is big.

Teaching With the Wearable

1. Invite students to help each other put on the aprons. For example, one child may hold the apron on his or her waist while the other child ties the ends of yarn together. Some students may need assistance tying.

2. Show the pictures of the pencil (both large and small). As a class, observe and compare them. Encourage students to use comparative language, such as *bigger than* and *smaller than* in their descriptions.

3. Ask students to examine their apron pockets. Ask: *How can we tell which pocket is for pictures of big things and which one is for small things?* (The word *big* is printed on the big pocket.) Ask: *What word is printed on the small pocket?* For younger students, draw attention to the relative size of the pockets. (The big pocket is larger than the small pocket.)

4. Model the process of using the pockets to sort pictures. Say: *This cookie looks bigger than the other cookie. I'm putting the big one in the big pocket of my apron. I'm putting the small cookie in the small pocket.*

5. Challenge students to sort their own sets of pictures. First, have children place pictures of similar objects next to each other (e.g., the big shell next to the small shell). Then, ask students to sort the pictures by size. For example, a child might place the keys pictures side by side and then determine which one is small and which is big.

6. Ask students to explain what they are doing and thinking as they sort. Ask: *Why did you put that key in your small pocket? How is this key different than the other key? How is it the same?*

7. Then, have each child place his or her sorted pictures into the corresponding apron pockets.

···● Extending Learning ●···

Room for More

Invite students to draw their very own pictures to place in their apron pockets. Ask children to draw small and big versions of the same object, such as a spoon, apple, or bowl. Encourage students to draw objects that are about the size of their small and big apron pockets (i.e., most real-life flowers [whether big or small] could fit in one of the children's apron pockets, a real-life house [of any size] could not). By using the sizes of their pockets as a guide, students will have an easier time comparing and sorting the big and small pictures they've drawn.

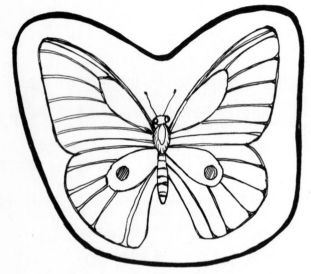

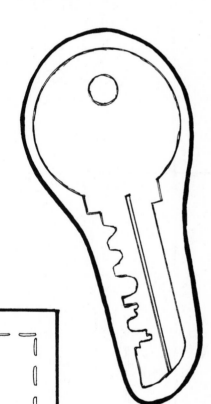

small

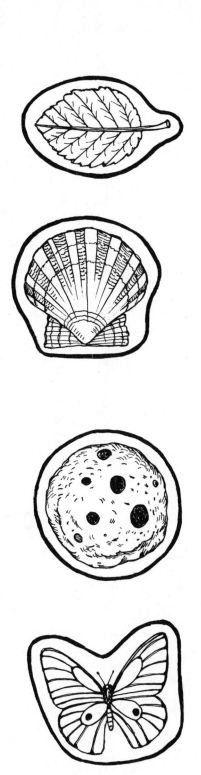

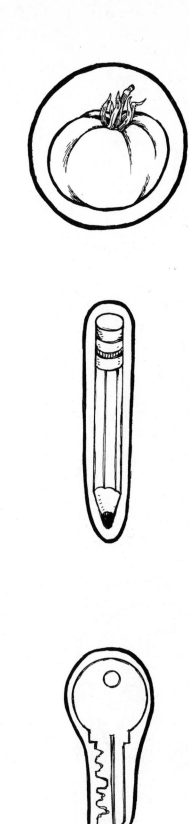

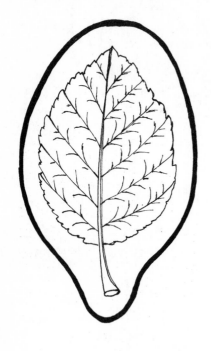

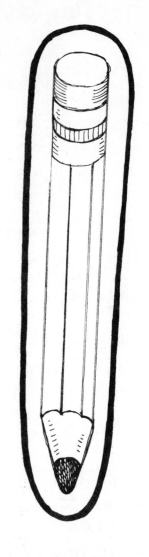

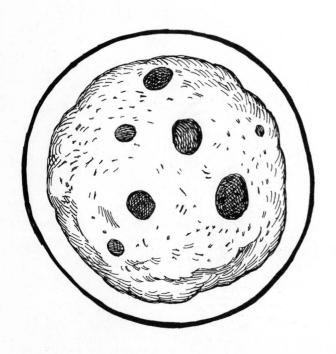

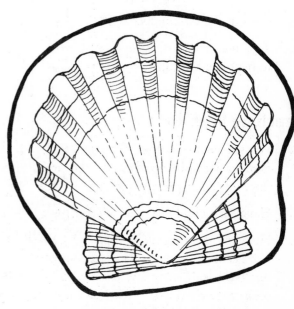

Adorable Wearables That Teach Early Concepts Scholastic Professional Books

Number Rings

Students make number rings they can use
as they count from one to ten.

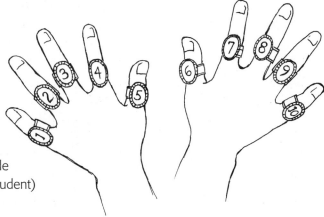

Materials

☼ copies of reproducible
  page 19 (for each student)

☼ scissors

☼ tape

☼ colored pencils, crayons, or markers (optional)

Making the Wearable

Make a model for yourself to use as a demonstration tool.
Then guide children in following these directions:

1. Color the number rings, if desired.

2. Cut out the ten number rings.

3. Tape the ends of each ring together
to fit students' fingers.

Teaching With the Wearable

1. Ask students to identify each of their fingers. Use terms children are
familiar with: thumb, pointer (or index finger), tall man (or middle
finger), ring finger, and pinky.

2. Have each child place his or her rings in a pile.

3. Hold up the 1-ring and ask students to find the same ring on their desks. As a
class, count the number of dots printed on the ring and say the word for that
number, *one*. Note: It is important that students place the 1-ring on their left
pinky to start, so that as they continue to place the rings in sequence, the
rings will read from left to right and in sequence from one to ten.

Skills

observing

identifying numerals

counting

ordering

Building Vocabulary

one

two

three

four

five

six

seven

eight

nine

ten

count

number

Book Links

My First Golden Book of 1, 2, 3 (Golden Books, 1999). Simple rhymes and puzzles make up the text that accompanies this introduction to numbers.

Try This!

Use number rings to help take attendance. As a class, determine which children are absent from school. Then, choose an Attendance Helper to put on his or her rings to show the number of children absent. For example, if Rosa, Donald, and Shavonne are absent, the Attendance Helper would need to hold up his or her left pinky, ring finger, and middle finger to show that three students are absent.

4. Place the ring on your left pinky and ask students to do the same. Note: Show students that the left thumb and index finger form a capital L. Encourage children to use this technique to check which hand is their left. For younger students, write a capital L on an index card. Invite children to match the thumb and pointer on their left hand to the L shape.

5. Hold up the 2-ring and repeat the process as above, but place the ring on the ring finger. Repeat, adding rings to each finger. When all the rings are on, the rings 1 to 5 will be on the left hand, from pinky to thumb. The rings 6 to 10 will be on the right hand, from thumb to pinky.

6. Encourage students to make connections between the words on their rings, the numerals, and the quantity of dots printed. Say: *Hold up the pointer-finger ring that has four dots on it. Count the dots.* Then ask: *What numeral is on this ring?* (4) *We counted four dots and now we know the numeral is 4. What word is printed on the ring?* (four) Repeat this process several times with different rings. Ask children to count the dots, identify the numeral, and say the number word.

7. Have students take off their rings, mix them up on their desks, and place them on their fingers in sequence again, from 1 to 10, pinky to pinky.

⋯●● Extending Learning ●●⋯

Counting Songs

Invite students to wear their number rings as the class sings counting songs and finger plays. Encourage children to hold up the finger that corresponds to the number in the song. For example, if the class is singing the counting song "Five Little Ducks," have students begin the song by holding up all the fingers on their left hands to show the rings numbered one through five. In this particular song, the baby ducks don't return to the mother initially. The number of ducks decreases by one at each chorus, until no ducks remain. (Children would need to indicate the decreasing number of ducks, at first showing their five rings, then four, three, two, one, and none.) In the final verse, all five ducks return to their mother. (Students would need to hold up all the ringed fingers on their left hand to indicate that the five ducks returned.) Songs that lend themselves to counting to five, like "Five Little Ducks," can readily be adapted for counting to ten, including "Three Green and Speckled Frogs," "This Old Man," and any of the counting songs sung to the tune of "Three Little Indians."

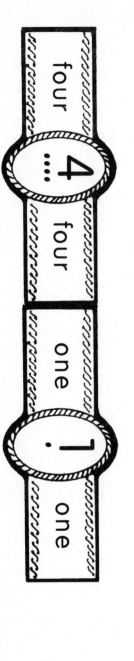

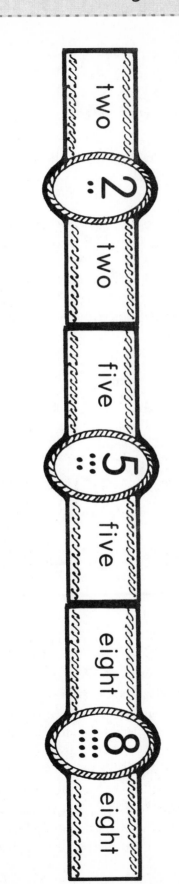

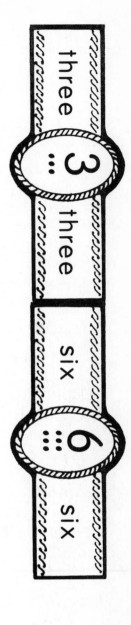

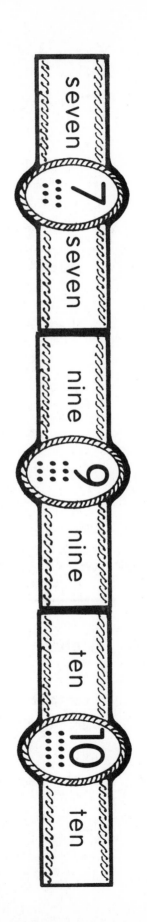

Garden-Harvest Colors Collar

Students make a collar to learn about colors.

Skills

observing
identifying
sorting
inferring

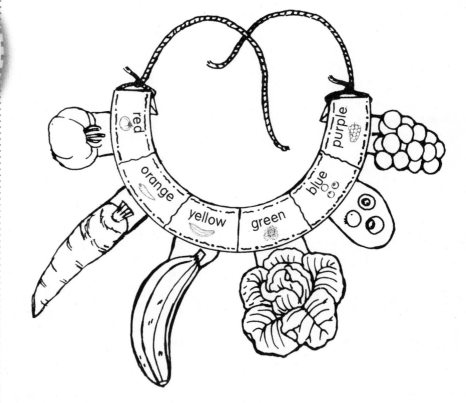

Building Vocabulary

banana
blue
blueberries
carrot
grapes
green
lettuce
orange
purple
red
tomato
yellow

Materials

- copies of reproducible pages 23 and 24 (for each student)
- one 24-inch piece of string or yarn (for each student)
- scissors
- tape
- colored pencils, crayons, or markers

Making the Wearable

Guide children in following these directions:

1. Cut out the collar segments and sorting pieces.

2. Position the two collar pieces side by side. Locate the tab next to the word *green*. Place it behind the section of collar labeled *yellow*. Tape the tab in place to secure.

3. Locate the tabs next to the words *red* and *purple*. Fold both tabs along the dashed lines, forming an enclosed area for yarn to pass through. Tape the tabs in place as shown.

4. Thread the ends of the yarn through the folded tabs.

5. Finish making and coloring the collar as part of the lesson below.

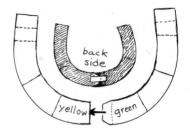
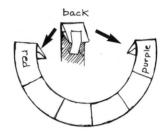
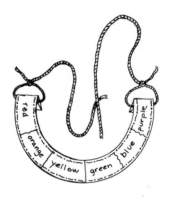

Teaching With the Wearable

1. Hold up the banana piece. Ask: *What color should we make this banana?* Encourage students to come to an agreement as to what color to make the banana (yellow).

2. Ask students to select a yellow crayon, colored pencil, or marker to color the banana. Repeat this process with the other picture pieces, agreeing upon the color: blueberries (blue), tomato (red), carrot (orange), lettuce (green), and grapes (purple). Tell students to use each color only once, thereby using a process of elimination.

3. Have students match their colored picture to the corresponding picture on the collar. Tell children to tape the pictures in place along the tab as shown.

Book Links

Colors by Robert Crowther (Candlewick Press, 2001). Flaps to lift and tabs to pull will intrigue students as they learn about colors.

4. Ask students to color the rectangular sections of the collar. Each section is labeled with a color word (red, orange, yellow, green, blue, purple). Ask: *How will we know what color to make each rectangle? What clues do we have?*

5. Place a collar around each student's neck. Use the loose ends of yarn to tie a bow, securing the collar loosely around the neck. Show children how to pull the yarn ends to loosen the bow and remove the collar easily.

6. Talk with students about the color of each fruit or vegetable. Student comments are likely to reflect a wide range of real-life experiences. After all, each of the items on the collar exists in a variety of natural colors. For example, yellow bananas are green before they're yellow. Then they turn brown! Grapes can be green, red, yellow, or purple.

Try This!

Teach students how primary colors make orange, green, and purple. Put separate containers of yellow and red tempera paint at an art center. Invite children to put on their smocks and paint. Ask: *What's happening to the colors as you paint? What color do the yellow and red make when you mix them together?* Discuss how yellow and red combine to make orange. Now make green! Provide containers of blue and yellow paint and observe as students make green. For extra fun, make purple by combining red and blue paint.

 Extending Learning

Rainbow Colors

Invite students to think about the colors of each object pictured. Ask: *What other colors have you seen tomatoes? bananas?* Photocopy a second set of pictures for each student. Have students color the objects with colors that reflect their real-life experience with those objects. For example, a child may color the grapes green because that's the color of the grapes at his or her home.

As a class, make a rainbow display that children can tape their pictures to easily. Tape single sheets of red, orange, yellow, green, blue, and purple construction paper side-by-side to form a rainbow. Then, invite students to match and then tape their pictures to the construction paper of the same color. When all the pictures are in place, title the display All the Colors on the Rainbow.

Student Page | Garden-Harvest Colors Collar

banana
red
orange
yellow
purple
blue
green
tape

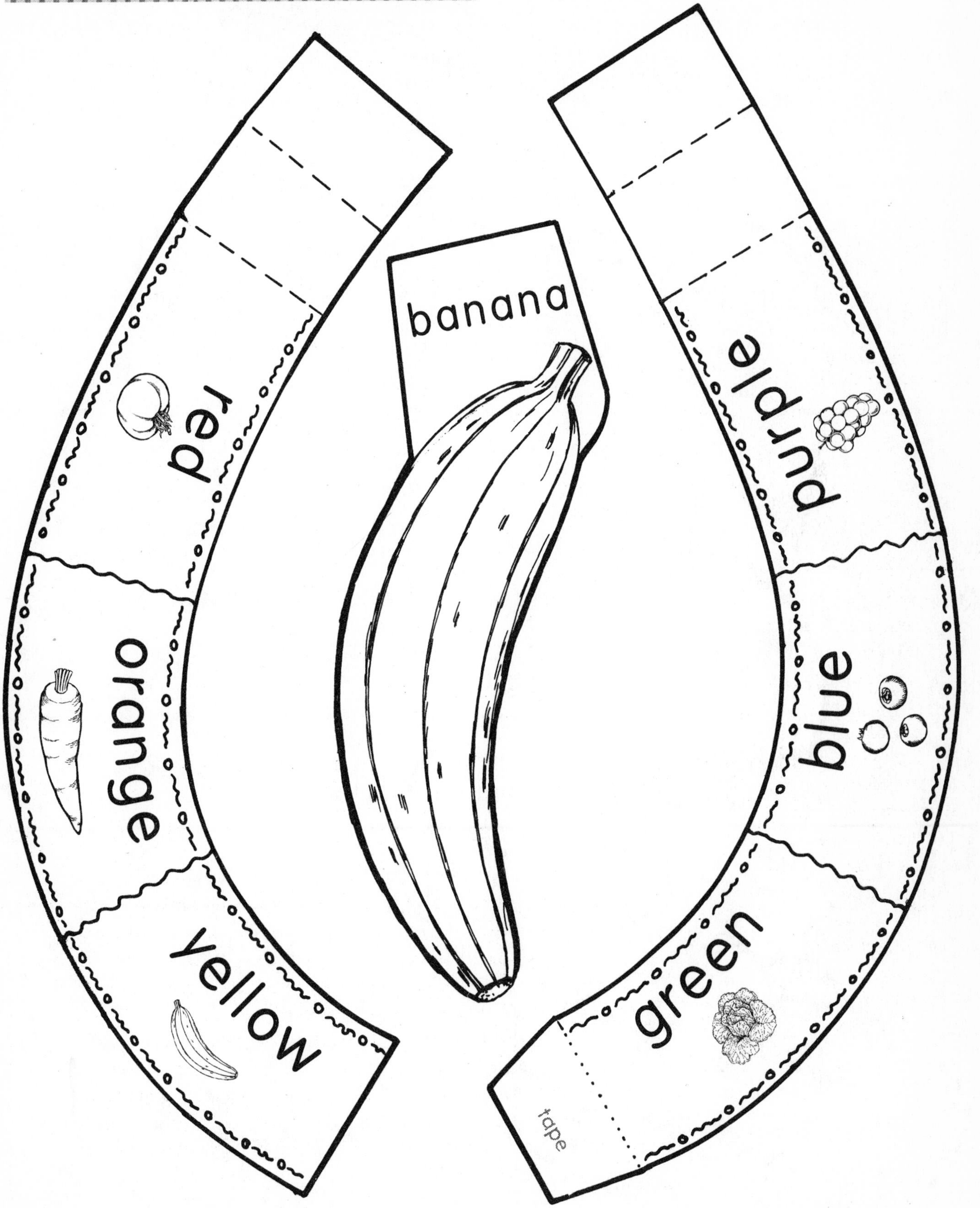

carrot

lettuce

tomato

grapes

blueberries

Adorable Wearables That Teach Early Concepts   Scholastic Professional Books

ABC Vest

Students make a vest that helps them learn to order, identify, and match the upper- and lowercase letters of the alphabet.

Materials

- ☼ copies of reproducible pages 27–29 (for each student)
- ☼ brown-paper grocery bag (for each student)
- ☼ scissors
- ☼ tape or glue sticks
- ☼ colored construction or copy paper
- ☼ colored pencils, crayons, or markers (optional)

Making the Wearable

Guide children in following these directions:

1. Cut open the front panel of the bag. Be sure to cut down the middle.

2. Cut a head opening in the bottom of the bag, which is facing up.

3. Cut arm openings in the sides of the bag.

4. Cut out the uppercase-letter strips on pages 27 and 28.

5. Attach the uppercase-letter strips on each half of the cut-open side of the bag. They fit best placed in rows across the vest, as shown. That way, children can read the letters in order from left to right.

Skills

observing
identifying
comparing
sequencing

Building Vocabulary

•••●●●•••

capital
curve
letter
line
lowercase
shape
straight
uppercase

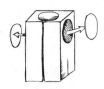

25

Try This!

When you make photocopies of the upper- and lowercase letters, copy them onto two different colored papers. For instance, you might photocopy all of the uppercase letters onto green paper and all of the lowercase letters onto yellow paper. That way, students will have an easier time keeping track of what they're matching and you'll have an easier time checking their developing skills.

Teaching With the Wearable

1. Invite students to make and wear their ABC vests.

2. Have each student cut out his or her own set of individual lowercase letters.

3. Divide the class into partners. Have pairs of students work together to match the lowercase letters to the corresponding uppercase (capital) letters on their partner's vest.

4. Encourage children to discuss the process of comparing and matching the upper- and lowercase letters. Ask: *How are they alike? How are they different?* Children may say, for example, that uppercase B has two curves while lowercase b has just one.

5. If you would like your students to permanently affix the lowercase letters to the uppercase letters on the vest as a record of their learning, provide students with tape or glue sticks. Ask students to remove their vests and attach the lowercase letters in place along the tabs of the uppercase letters as shown.

Extending Learning

Mix 'n Match

Photocopy a set of the lowercase letters, cut them out, and mix them in a bowl. Challenge a student to pick and identify a letter, then orient the letter right side up and forward. Ask other students to point to the corresponding uppercase letter on their own vests, or on the vest of the child seated beside them.

Lowercase Lookouts

Add one more fun job to the Classroom Helpers' chart! Invite one or two students to be Lowercase Lookouts and tell them that with this job their ABC vest is a kind of uniform! The Lookout's job is to be on the lookout for lowercase letters wherever the class goes—on bulletin boards, in the library, on signs in the hallways, or anywhere there is environmental print. Have the Lookouts keep a tally of the lowercase letters they find. You might consider creating an alphabet checklist template that students can check off when it's their turn to be the Lowercase Lookouts.

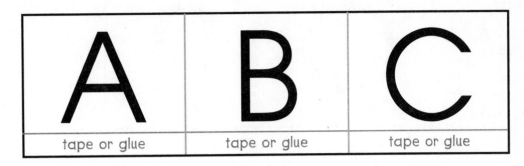

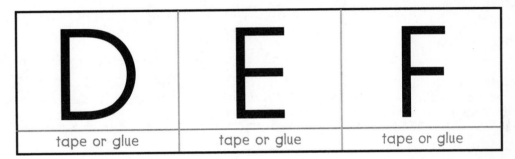

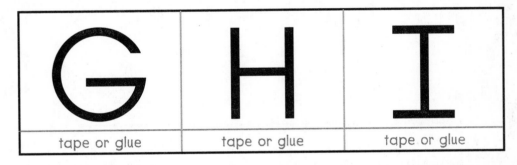

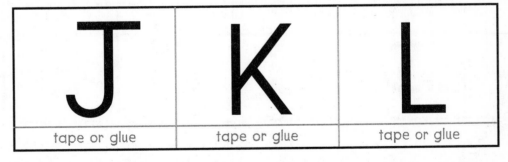

ABC Vest

P	Q	R
tape or glue	tape or glue	tape or glue

S	T	U	V
tape or glue	tape or glue	tape or glue	tape or glue

W	X	Y	Z
tape or glue	tape or glue	tape or glue	tape or glue

a	b	c	d	e

f	g	h	i	j

Adorable Wearables That Teach Early Concepts   Scholastic Professional Books

ABC Vest

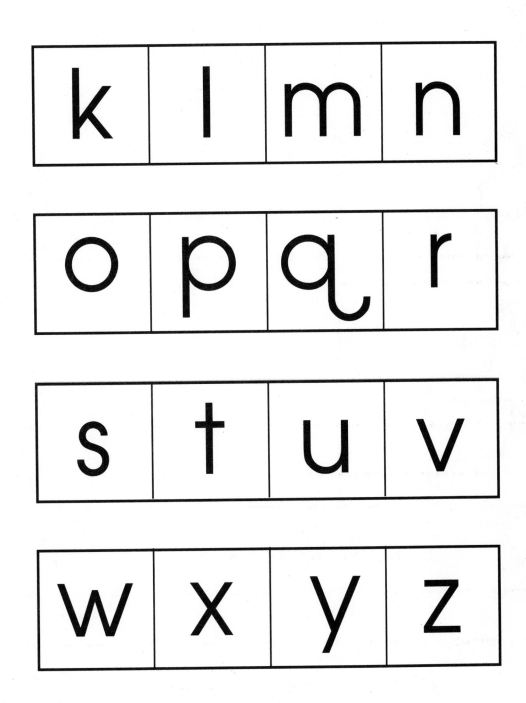

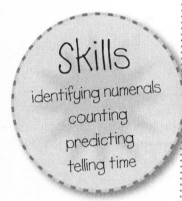

Tell-the-Time Wristwatch

Students make a wristwatch to learn about measuring time.

Building Vocabulary

●●●●● ●● ●●●●●

alarm

clock

digital

hands

hour

midnight

minute

noon

o'clock

second

time

watch

wrist

Materials

☼ copies of reproducible page 33 (for each student)

☼ brass fastener (for each student)

☼ 6-inch circle of colored construction paper (for each student, optional)

☼ scissors

☼ tape or glue sticks

☼ colored pencils, crayons, or markers (optional)

Making the Wearable

Guide children in following these directions:

1. Color the watch parts, if desired.

2. Cut out the watch face, hands, and wristband.

3. Position the watch face so it's face up on the construction paper circle (optional). Tape or glue in place.

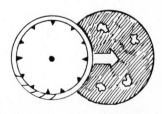

4. Place the short arrow on top of the long arrow, so the rounded end and the arrow points match up.

5. Center the rounded ends on top of the black dot of the watch face. Hold the arrows in place.

6. Position the wristband under the watch face, lining up the black dots. If you're using the colored construction paper circle, center the watch face over the circle.

7. Push the brass fastener tabs through the rounded-end of the arrows, the watch face, the construction-paper circle (if you're using it), and the watchband. Fold the fastener tabs back to secure all the pieces in place.

8. Tape the ends of the watchband together, large enough for a child to fit a hand through.

Teaching With the Wearable

1. Invite students to wear their wristwatches.

2. Ask children to tell you what they know about telling time. Ask: *Where have you seen clocks? How do members of your family know when to wake in the morning? Why do you think people use clocks to figure out what time it is?*

3. Discuss why people use clocks. Explain that, as rulers measure how long an object is with inches and feet, clocks help people measure time with minutes and hours.

4. Show students how to turn the arrows on the watch face in a clockwise direction. The arrows pass the numbers in sequence from smallest to largest, from numbers 1 to 12.

5. Explain that the arrows are called hands. The long arrow is called the minute hand because it measures minutes. The short arrow is called the hour hand. Ask: *Why do you think it is called the hour hand?*

6. Ask students to set their watches to 1 o'clock, placing the minute hand on the twelve and the hour hand on the one. To help younger

Book Links

It's About Time by Dina Anastasio (Grosset Dunlap, 1993). Clear, simple directions will help teach students how to tell time on the book's big watch face.

children manipulate the hour hand with ease, tape the minute hand in place at the twelve. That way, only the hour hand is moveable. Then, ask students to predict where the hour hand needs to be to show 2 o'clock, 3 o'clock, and so on.

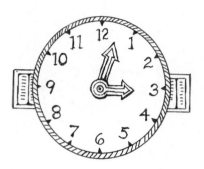

··● Extending Learning ●··

Set Your Watches!

Every hour on the hour, tell students to set their watches. Use the classroom clock or an instructional clock to show where the hour hands need to be placed. Ask students to predict what time it will be in an hour. Or, ask them to tell you what time it was exactly an hour ago. For extra fun, set an alarm clock to buzz in an hour . . . and set your watches when you hear it. If you're using a digital alarm clock, challenge students to set their wristwatches to the hour they see on the digital clock.

Kid-Sized Clocks

Turn an old sheet or tablecloth into a GIANT clock face. Just cut the cloth into a circle, draw a dot in the center, mark off the hours, and add the numbers 1 to 12. Choose one student to be the hour-hand helper and another to be the minute-hand helper. Challenge students to examine the classroom wall clock and arrange their bodies on the floor to match the wall clock. Invite the rest of the class to assist the clock-hand helpers in finding the correct positions. For example, if it is 2 o'clock the minute-hand helper will lay his or her body straight between the twelve and the dot in the center of the clock face. The hour-hand helper will lay his or her body straight between the numeral two and the dot in the center. As a class, tell the time!

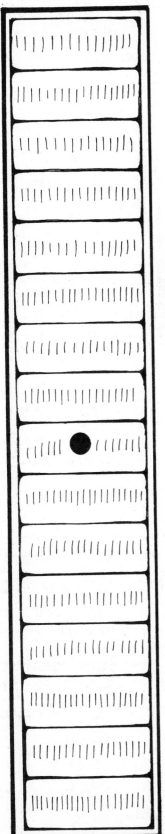

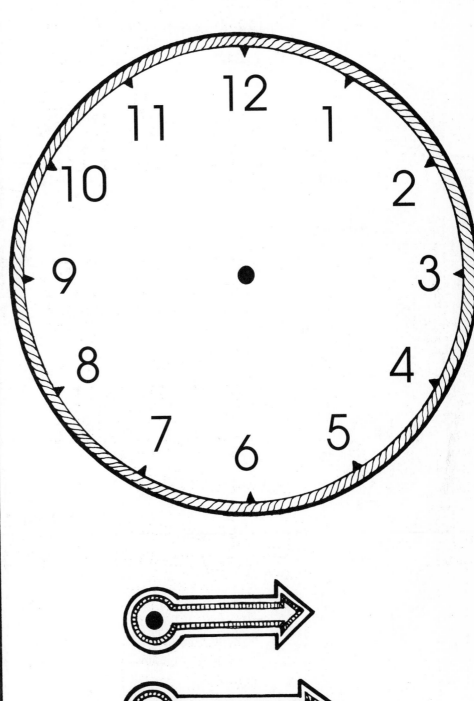

Month-by-Month Belt

Students learn about the months of the year by making a lift-the-flap belt.

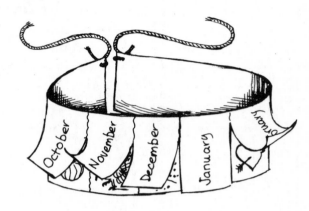

Skills

identifying month names

sequencing

communicating

inferring

Materials

- copies of reproducible pages 36–38 (for each student)
- two 12-inch pieces of yarn (for each student)
- one-hole punch
- scissors
- tape
- colored pencils, crayons, or markers (optional)

Making the Wearable

Guide children in following these directions:

1. Cut out the month panel and corresponding picture panel on each page. Also cut slits along the solid black lines between the month names.

2. Place each month-name panel on top of its picture panel. Tape along the top edge, so that the month flaps can be lifted to reveal the month-related pictures beneath.

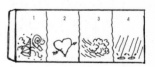

3. Check to be sure the numbers on the lower right corner of the month and picture flaps match. For example, the August flap has the number eight printed on it and so does its corresponding picture.

4. Finish making the wearable as part of the lesson. Then, color the panels, if desired.

Building Vocabulary

January
February
March
April
May
June
July
August
September
October
November
December

34

Teaching With the Wearable

1. Ask students to place their panels in front of them. Tell them that the belt begins with the first month of the year. Ask: *What is the first month of a year? Which picture goes with that word?*

2. Invite children to think of strategies for determining what the words on the belt say. For example, students could lift the flaps to see what clues the pictures offer, order the months based on the numerals printed in the bottom right corner of the flaps, compare the words on the panels to the words on a classroom calendar, sing a song that lists the months in sequence, and so on.

3. Have children place the three four-month panels in sequence, from January to December.

4. Ask students to flip the panels over and tape them together forming a belt.

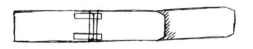

5. Locate the dots printed on the front of the January and December panels. At each dot, punch holes for the string to pass through.

6. Tie both pieces of yarn to the belt at the holes.

7. Have each student hold the belt to his or her waist. Tie the yarn into a bow to secure.

Jump for Joy: A Book of Months by Megan Halsey (Bradbury Press, 1994). The alliterative text and irresistible paper-cut illustrations make this concept book fun to read again and again.

Try This!

Make a belt just for the class-room. Place it beside the class calendar. Each day, invite one student to put on the belt and become the class Month Minder. Challenge the Month Minder to point to the month flap that corresponds to the name of the current calendar month and then lift the flap to reveal the picture. Invite him or her to share information about the month with classmates. For example, the Month Minder could identify school holidays, field trips, characteristic weather, and so on.

·· ● **Extending** Learning ● ·····

Pictures Around the Year

Divide the class into small groups. Invite students to put on their belts and take turns naming the months and lifting the flaps to reveal the corresponding pictures. Challenge children to use what they know about each month, explaining to other group members what each picture shows about each month. For example, a child may point to the January flap and say: *January.* He or she could lift the flap to show the party blowers and say: *January has a picture of party blowers because New Year's Day is the first day of the year.* Encourage children to take turns until all twelve months have been named and their pictures explained.

tape

January 1

1

February 2

2

March 3

3

April 4

4

tape

May

5

5

June

6

6

July

7

7

August

8

8

tape

September 9

9

October 10

10

November 11

11

December 12

12

All-Weather Mittens

Students make mittens they can use to identify different types of weather and weather words.

sunny

Skills

communicating

comparing

describing

inferring

Materials

☀ copies of reproducible pages 41 and 42 (for each student)

☀ scissors

☀ tape or glue sticks

☀ construction paper

☀ colored pencils, crayons, or markers (optional)

Making the Wearable

Guide children in following these directions:

1. Color the mitten parts, if desired.

2. Cut out the piece on each page and fold along the center line.

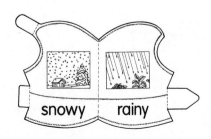

snowy   rainy

Building Vocabulary

chilly

cloudy

cold

cool

hot

rainy

snowy

sunny

warm

windy

39

3. Tape the arrow tab on each piece over the corresponding square tab on that piece.

4. Tape the other tab over the top of each mitten.

5. Fit the mittens over students' hands. Note: Students with small hands may be able to fit their fingers inside the mittens in a traditional manner. Children with larger hands may wear the mittens with their fingers slipped through the top.

Teaching With the Wearable

1. Invite students to put on their mittens.

2. Read the words under the picture on each mitten. Challenge children to compare the pictures. Ask: *How are they alike? How are they different?*

3. Invite students to use what they know to infer which season is the most likely to have the weather shown in each picture. Answers will vary depending on the climate where you teach.

Book Links

Little Cloud by Eric Carle (Philomel, 1996). Follow the adventures of a small cloud for a quick and easy lesson on the water cycle.

Try This!

Write a class weather report! Peer out the window or take a walk out to the playground. Record student predictions and observations on chart paper. Be sure to underline or highlight all the weather words. Consider adding illustrations to key weather words. Younger students will enjoy having the rebus-style support. Older students will have fun creating illustrations for words they recognize.

⋯•● Extending Learning ●•⋯

Weather Helpers

Each day invite your students to slip on their mittens and become Weather Helpers. Challenge students to refer to the illustrations on their mittens and their corresponding weather words as they describe the weather outside (rainy, snowy, sunny, cloudy). For example, a student who sees the sun shining outside might hold up his or her mitten, point to the word sunny or the sunny illustration, and say, "It's sunny outside." Invite that student to elaborate, sharing further observations about the weather. Ask open-ended questions, such as: *What did you notice about the temperature outside? Why did you wear a jacket to school today? What other clothing items did you wear?* (boots, scarf, hat)

sunny

cloudy

rainy

snowy

Adorable Wearables That Teach Early Concepts   Scholastic Professional Books

Plants-and-Animals Necklace

Students make a necklace to learn about plants and animals.

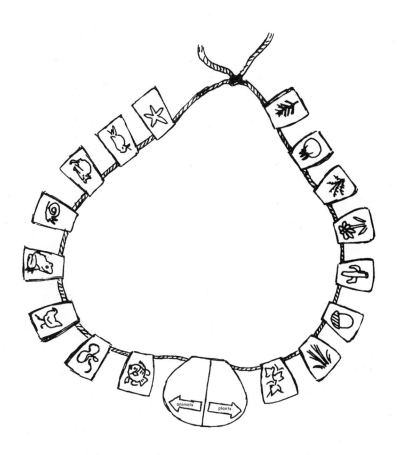

Skills

observing
sorting
classifying

Building Vocabulary

acorn
bird
cactus
cat
chicken
fern
fish
flower
frog
grass
pine tree
snail
snake
starfish
tomato
vine

Materials

☼ copies of reproducible pages 46–48 (for each student)

☼ 18-inch piece of yarn (for each student)

☼ scissors

☼ tape

☼ colored pencils, crayons, or markers (optional)

Making the Wearable

Guide children in following these directions:

1. Color the pieces of the necklace, if desired.

2. Cut out all the pieces and fold along the dashed lines.

3. Tape each piece along the three sides.

4. Thread the yarn through the piece with the words "animals" and "plants" printed on it. Position this piece (or medallion) so that equal lengths of yarn extend from both sides.

5. Finish making the necklace as part of the lesson below.

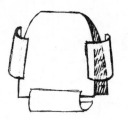

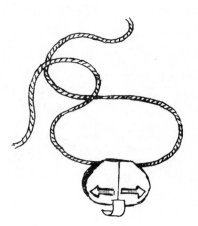

Book Links

A Tree Is a Plant by Clyde Robert Bulla. Let's Read and Find Out series. (HarperCollins, 1960). Colorful illustrations and simple informative text make it easy to understand why this title has remained in print so long.

The Life-size Animal Opposites Book (DK Publications, 1994). This well-illustrated book uses animals to help students learn about opposites.

Teaching With the Wearable

1. Ask students: *How can we tell whether something is an animal or a plant?*

2. As a class, discuss the similarities and differences between animals and plants. Here is some information to get you started:

   Animals are living things that can move from place to place. Most animals have legs, heads, eyes, mouths, and so on. Some have wings, shells, feathers, or fur. Animals cannot make their own food; they eat plants or other animals.

   Plants are living things that grow in soil. They have leaves, stems, and roots. Most plants grow flowers and have fruit. Some have nuts or seeds. Others have cones. Plants make their own food and cannot move from one place to another.

3. Tell children that whenever they wear their necklaces, they become detectives. The class' first assignment is to determine which of the necklace pictures show animals and which show plants.

4. Have students place their medallion in front of them so the medallion is in the center of their work space. Note: It is important that students

place the medallion so that the words are right-side up, with "animals" on the left and "plants" on the right. Ask: *What do you think the arrows mean? Where should we put the pictures of animals? plants?*

5. Have children sort their pieces into two groups—with the pictures of animals on the left and plants on the right (as indicated by the arrows).

6. Tell children to thread the yarn through the animal pieces. Then have children do the same with the plant pieces. When complete, the necklace should have pictures of animals to the left of the "animals" arrow and plant pictures to the right of the "plants" arrow.

7. Tie the ends of the yarn so students can easily slip the necklace over their heads. Show students how their necklace can be worn two ways, with the pictures showing or the animal and plant names showing.

···● **Extending** Learning ●···

Show and Share

Challenge students to bring in a picture of an animal and a plant not shown on their necklaces. (Old nature magazines and garden catalogs work well for this activity.) Ask each child to talk about the picture he or she has selected. Ask: *Why did you choose that picture? How did you know whether it was a picture of an animal or a plant?* Then, take this activity one step further. Collect the pictures and place them at a sorting center. Make a T-chart on a piece of oaktag. On the left side, write the word *animals* and draw a left-facing arrow. On the right side, write the word *plants* and draw a right-facing arrow. Invite students wear their necklaces as an instant plant and animal reference as they sort their classmates' pictures. Have children place the animal pictures on the left side and plants on the right side of the T-chart.

Try This!

Take a nature walk! Invite students to put on their necklaces and join you in a search for animals and plants. (Playgrounds and local parks are great for this activity.) If a student sees an object not pictured on the necklace, invite the child to choose a friend to help determine whether the object is an animal or a plant. Back in the classroom, invite students to draw pictures of the animals and plants they encountered on the walk.

flower

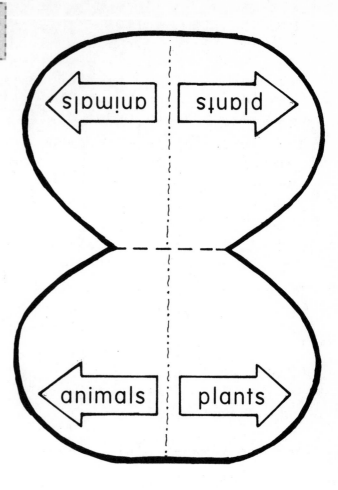

animals plants

animals plants

bird

cat

snail

frog

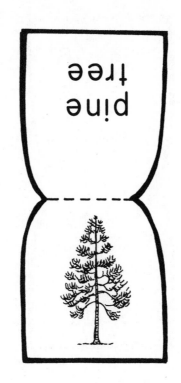

pine
tree

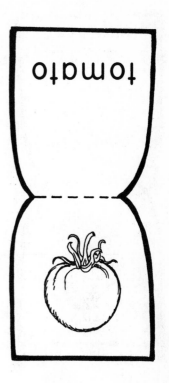

tomato

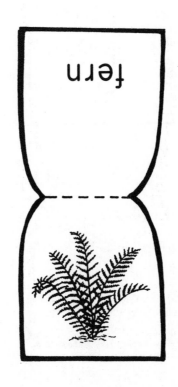

starfish

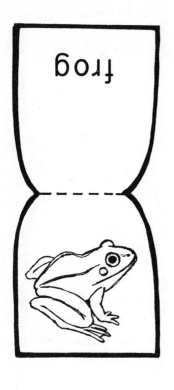

fern

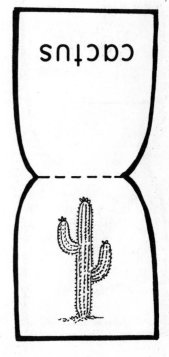

cactus

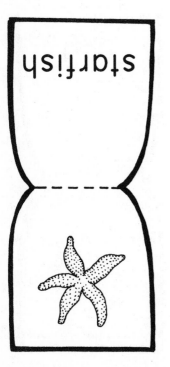

Plants-and-Animals
Necklace

acorn

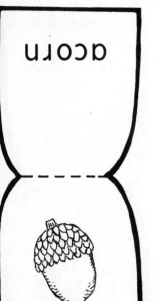

grass

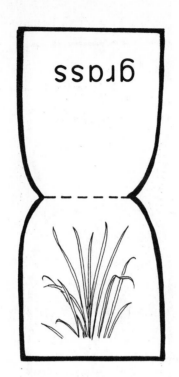

chicken

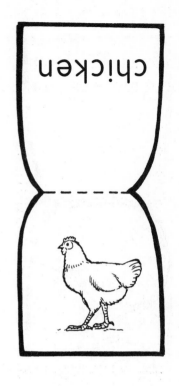

snake

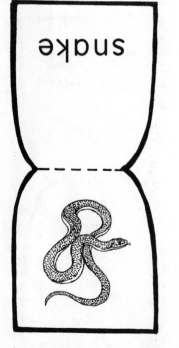

vine

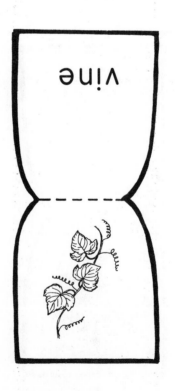

fish

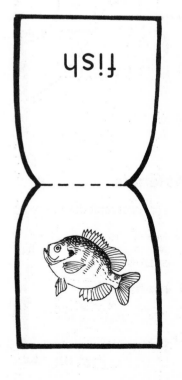

Five-Senses Mask

Students make a mask they can use to learn about their five senses.

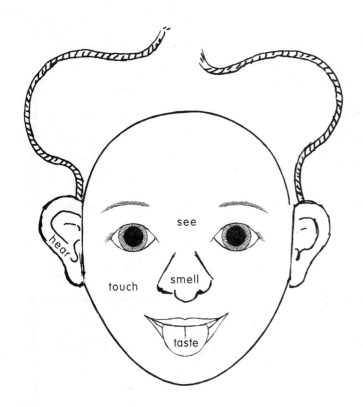

Skills
observing
identifying
inferring

Building Vocabulary

ears
eyes
body
feel
hear
nose
see
smell
taste
touch

Materials

※ copies of reproducible pages 52 and 53 (for each student)
※ two 12-inch pieces of yarn (for each student)
※ scissors
※ one-hole punch
※ tape
※ colored pencils, crayons, or markers (optional)

Making the Wearable

Guide children in following these directions:

1. Color the mask, if desired.

2. Cut out the mask, nose, and ears.

3. Cut a hole in each iris for pupils.

4. Cut along the lines where the nose will be, making slits for the nose tabs to pass through.

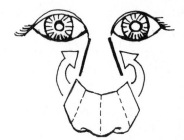

5. Fold the nose down the middle and along the tabs. Insert the tabs into the nose slits on the mask. Turn the mask over and tape the tabs in place.

6. Fold the ears along the tabs. Tape both ears to the front of the mask to secure their position.

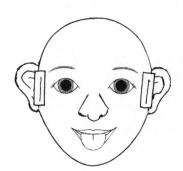

7. Locate the dots printed on the tabs for both the ears and mask. At each dot, punch holes for the yarn to pass through.

8. Tie both pieces of yarn to the mask at the holes.

9. Have each student hold the mask on his or her face. Tie the yarn into a bow to secure.

Teaching With the Wearable

1. Invite students to wear their masks. Tell children that the masks they've made will help them learn about their five senses.

2. Discuss how different parts of our bodies help us make observations about our environment. Then, have children point out the parts of their body that help them see, hear, smell, and taste things in the world around them (eyes, ears, nose, tongue). For example, say: *Point to the part on your face that helps you see. Now, point to the part of your body that helps you hear.*

Book Links

Sing Along and Learn by Ken Sheldon (Scholastic, 1997). Twelve learning songs with reproducible activity pages teach primary skills and concepts, including the five senses.

3. Invite students to talk about the sense of touch. Ask: *What happens when you touch something? What do you learn about it?* Students may say, for example, that they can feel temperature, texture, and moisture.

4. Although we may associate touch with fingers, invite children wearing the Senses Mask to explore the sense of touch using the skin on their faces. For a hands-on experience, ask students to lightly touch their own cheeks with a crayon. Encourage children to discuss how it feels on their skin. For example, students may say the crayon feels cool, waxy, and dry.

·•◐ **Extending** Learning ◑•·

Mystery Box

Play a favorite classroom game like Mystery Box, a sensory game that invites students to use the sense of touch to describe an object they can't see, hear, or smell. But this time, take Mystery Box a step further. After the student whose turn it is identifies the object, ask the child to use his or her other senses to describe the object. (For safety and hygiene reasons, don't have children taste objects.)

To make a Mystery Box, cut an old sock off at the ankle. Staple or glue it over the opening on an empty top-dispensing tissue box. (Students will need to place their hands into the tube of the sock to reach into the box, so secure the sock well.) Then, gather small objects that students may know the feel of, for instance building blocks, dollhouse furniture, pencils, and leaves. Be sure to include objects in a variety of shapes and textures.

When the class is ready to play, have students put on their masks. Then, model what you expect the students to do. Reach into the box and grasp an object. Tell them you're thinking about what the object could be and some words that might describe it. If the object is a leaf, you might say: *It feels smooth and papery. It feels like something in my mother's garden, so I'm going to guess that this object is a leaf. Pull the leaf out and show it.* Then say: *My eyes help me see that this leaf is yellow and orange. My ears help me hear a quiet sound when I rub its surface. My nose helps me remember that this leaf smells like the woods after a rain.* Talking through the observation process in this way will help children think about the senses they use every day to identify objects in their world.

Try This!

Have your students put on their masks. Tell them that when they wear their masks, their senses are keener. Their ears can hear even the tiniest of sounds! Ask children to listen to the sounds in the classroom and raise one hand if they hear something they want their classmates to notice. For example, a child may hear a bird outside the window or a student's footsteps receding down the hall. Encourage children to be as quiet as caterpillars (or butterflies) as they listen to the quiet.

51

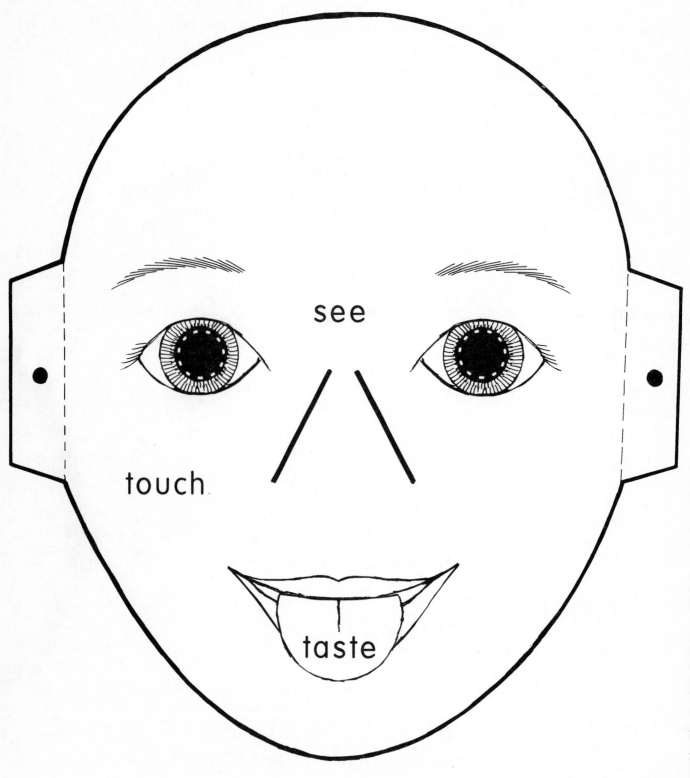

see

touch.

taste

Adorable Wearables That Teach Early Concepts   Scholastic Professional Books

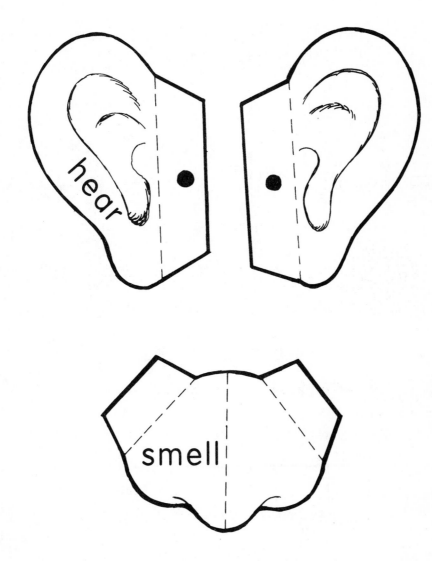

Transportation Shin Guards

Students make transportation shin guards and learn how people move from place to place.

Skills

identifying

classifying

comparing

sorting

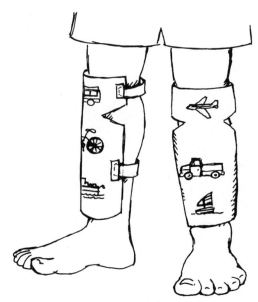

Building **Vocabulary**

●■● ● ● ●■●

air

airplane

bicycle

bus

land

sailboat

ship

truck

water

Materials

☼ copies of reproducible pages 56 and 57 (for each student)

☼ scissors

☼ tape

☼ colored pencils, crayons, or markers (optional)

Making the Wearable

Guide children in following these directions:

1. Cut out both shin guards and the four paper bands (strips).

2. Tape one band to the upper section and one band to the lower section of each shin guard.

3. Have children place their shin guards on both of their shins. Then show them how to overlap the bands and tape them in place.

Teaching With the Wearable

1. While wearing their shin guards, ask students how they use their legs to move from place to place (walk, run, climb, jump, swim, bike ride, roller blade, and so on).

2. Discuss how people use vehicles to move from place to place.

3. As a class, identify the vehicles on both shin guards.

4. Challenge students to say where each kind of transportation is found (land, sea, and air). For example, a child could say: *An airplane travels in the air. A truck travels on land.*

Boats and Planes by Byron Burton (HarperCollins, 1986). Both books provide an introduction to boats and planes as means of transportation.

···● Extending Learning ●···

All Aboard!

Make several copies of the shin guards and cut out the pictures. Set the pictures aside. Tell students that they will be making a pictograph to show which vehicles children in the class have used as a means of transportation. To set up the graph, glue each vehicle's picture in a column along the vertical axis. Point to the different vehicles on the shin guards. Tell children that if they have traveled in that type of vehicle, they should raise their hand and then come up and select the vehicle's picture. Have children glue the pictures in rows along the horizontal axis of the graph. For example, if six children have traveled on an airplane, each of those children would need to glue a picture of an airplane on the airplane row. Once the graph is complete, invite students to discuss the results.

Classifying Vehicles

Divide the class into three groups. Have each group make a poster for sorting and classifying vehicles. Provide students with oak tag and tempera paint. Have them paint a land scene, a sea scene, and an air scene. Allow the posters to dry overnight. Then, make a copy of both shin guards and cut out the pictures. Invite students to match each vehicle with the poster scenes. For example, a child could put all the boats on the sea poster, all the planes on the air poster, and all the ground vehicles on the land poster.

Try This!

Make vehicles from recycled containers. Invite students to bring in cardboard boxes, plastic lids, and bottle caps. Place the materials at an art table. Tell the class it's their job to turn the recycled materials into vehicles using glue and their imaginations. Allow the vehicles to dry overnight, then have children use paint, tissue paper, pipe cleaners, and other craft materials to complete the vehicles. Invite students to name their creations. For example, a child who has made a bicycle might name it "My Recycled Bicycle."

tape

tape

tape

tape

tape

tape

tape

tape

Common Cents Bracelets

Students make bracelets and learn about United States coins.

Skills

identifying

classifying

comparing

observing

Materials

☼ copies of reproducible pages 60–64 (for each student to have a "heads" and a "tails" version of all four coins, 8 bracelets in total)

☼ 12 pennies

☼ 12 nickels

☼ 12 dimes

☼ 12 quarters

☼ scissors

☼ tape

☼ colored pencils, crayons, or markers (optional)

Making the Wearable

Guide children in following these directions:

1. Color the eight bracelet strips, if desired.

2. Cut out the bracelet strips.

3. Tape each of the bracelet strips end-to-end to fit around either wrist, with the coins facing outward. The bracelets may be worn in any order.

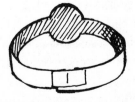

Building Vocabulary

bracelet

change

coin

dime

money

nickel

penny

quarter

Teaching With the Wearable

1. Divide the class into small groups. Give each group of children several pennies, nickels, dimes, and quarters to handle and examine.

2. Hold up a penny and invite each group of students to find a coin like it in their coin pile.

3. Invite them to describe the coin. Ask questions, such as: *What numbers do we see on it? What pictures are on it? How does this coin look different than the other coins?*

4. Invite students to identify each coin by name (penny, nickel, dime, and quarter).

5. Ask students to match the coins on their money bracelets to the actual coins. Encourage them to examine the images, numbers, and words on the front and back of each coin.

The Painted Pig by Elizabeth Morrow (University of New Mexico Press, 2001). This book, first published in 1930, uses delightful storytelling and vibrant illustrations to tell the tale of a painted pig.

Try This!

Make piggy banks! Ask parents to send in sturdy containers with plastic lids. (Oatmeal containers work well for this activity.) Use scissors or a box cutter to make a hole in each container plastic lid, a hole large enough for students to fit quarters through easily. Invite students to paint their containers with tempera paints. When dry, have children add details like googlie eyes and pipe-cleaner tails. Then, encourage students to have fun saving pennies in their piggy banks!

··●● **Extending** Learning ●●··

Change Exchange

Make multiple copies of each coin bracelet and help students learn coin equivalents. To teach the value of a nickel, have each student in one group wear five penny bracelets and each student in the other group wear a nickel bracelet. Say: *If you're wearing five pennies on your wrist, look for a classmate wearing a nickel bracelet. His or her nickel is worth your five pennies.* Both children raise their hands when a match has been found. For dimes, match ten penny bracelets with a dime bracelet. For quarters, match 25 penny bracelets with a quarter bracelet. If the class is ready, continue to match coin equivalents. For example, children could match two nickels for a dime, two dimes and one nickel for a quarter, and so on.

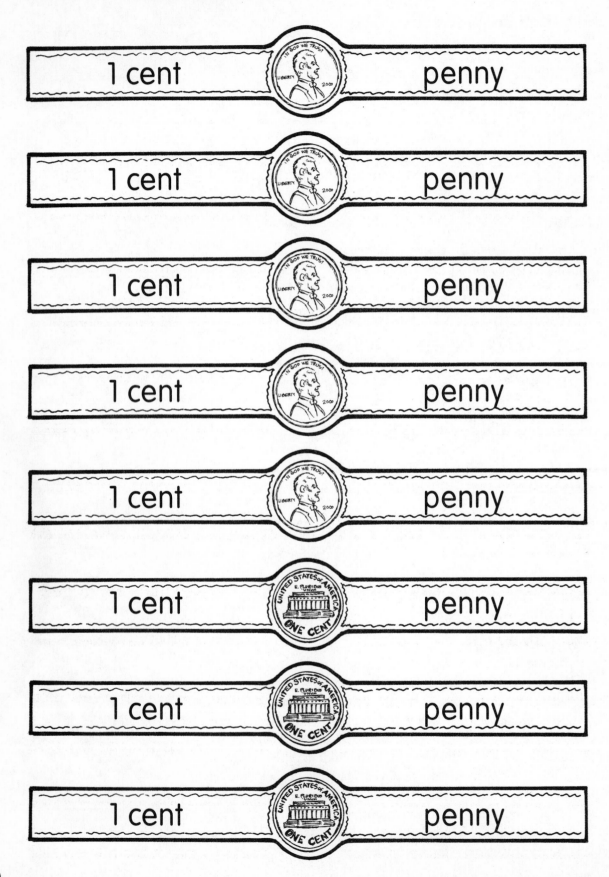

1 cent   penny

1 cent   penny

1 cent   penny

1 cent   penny

1 cent   penny

1 cent   penny

1 cent   penny

1 cent   penny

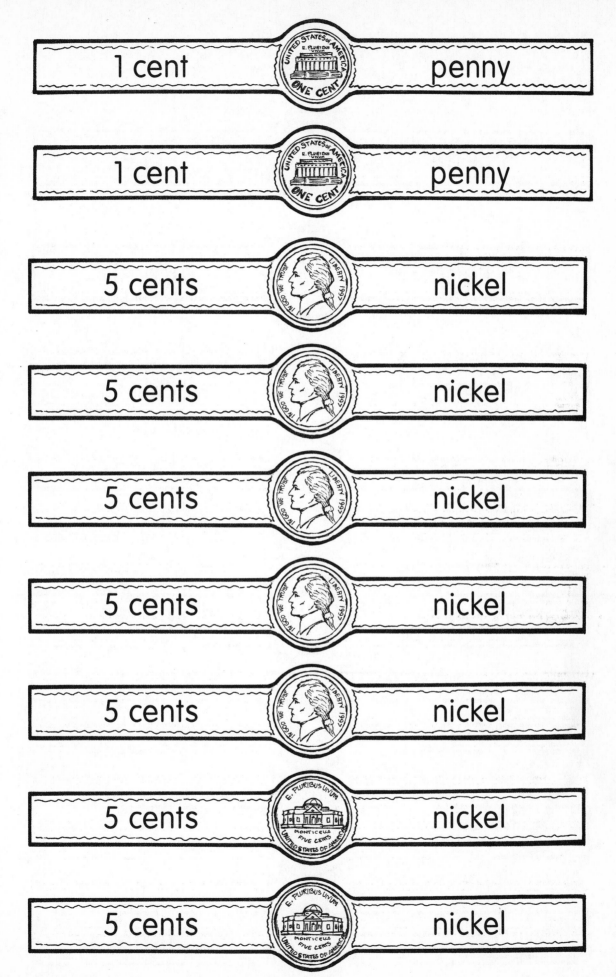

1 cent   penny

1 cent   penny

5 cents   nickel

5 cents   nickel

5 cents   nickel

5 cents   nickel

5 cents   nickel

5 cents   nickel

5 cents   nickel

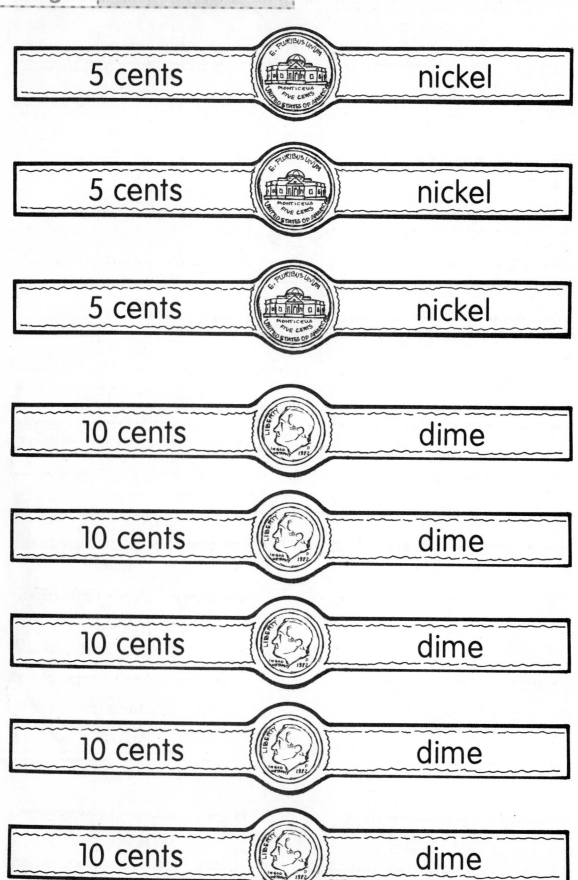

5 cents   nickel

5 cents   nickel

5 cents   nickel

10 cents   dime

10 cents   dime

10 cents   dime

10 cents   dime

10 cents   dime

Adorable Wearables That Teach Early Concepts   Scholastic Professional Books

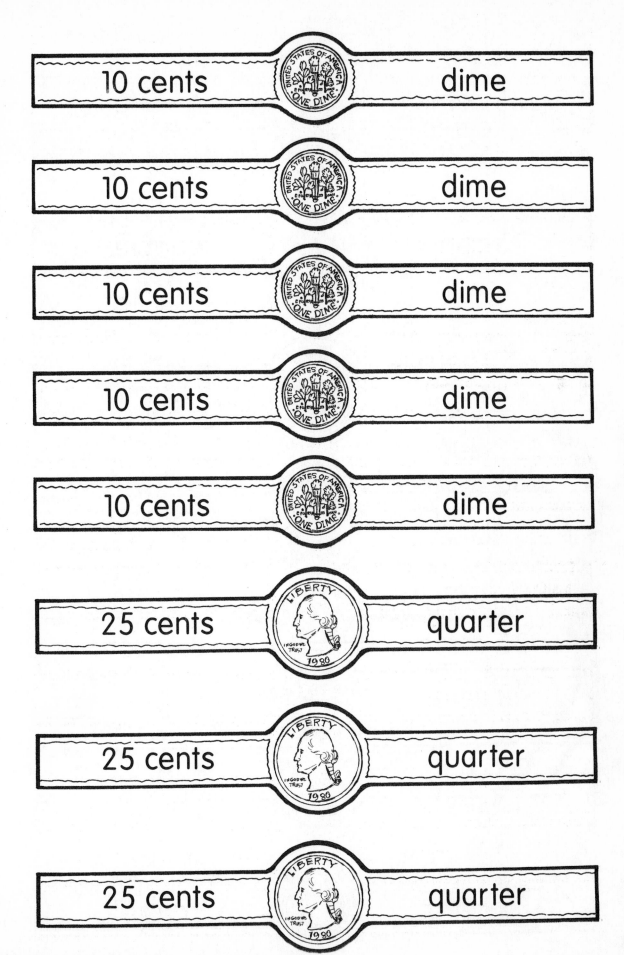

10 cents   dime

10 cents   dime

10 cents   dime

10 cents   dime

10 cents   dime

25 cents   quarter

25 cents   quarter

25 cents   quarter

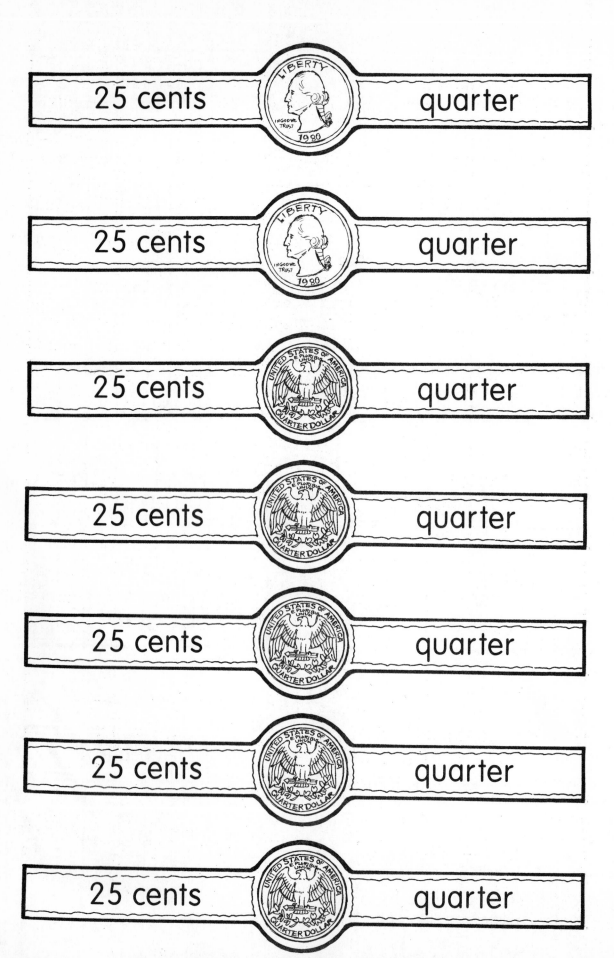

25 cents — quarter

25 cents — quarter

25 cents — quarter

25 cents — quarter

25 cents — quarter

25 cents — quarter

25 cents — quarter

Adorable Wearables That Teach Early Concepts   Scholastic Professional Books